40 DAYS OF PRAYER

*For Our Personal Growth,
and Our Nation*

D1225757

NATE KINGSBURY

AWAKE: 40 Days of Prayer

Copyright 2020 by Nate Kingsbury

All Bible verses are taken from the *Holy Bible, New International Version*. NIV. Copyright 1973, 1978, 1984 by International Bible Society. All rights reserved.

Designed by Sarah Snyder.
Published and printed in the United States of America.

Special Thanks

I am so thankful that the Lord prompted me to write this devotional, and I feel so honored to have a team of people who were willing to help make it possible. I can write and have ideas, but everything else that goes into compiling, editing, and publishing a book requires other people's gifts to complete.

I personally want to thank Sarah Snyder, who helped handle all aspects of this project, including the designing, publishing, and revision of this book, and who really encouraged me to make this project bigger than what I imagined it to be. Special thanks to all the staff members and church attendees who spent time proofreading and praying over this book.

I am also grateful for my wife and my children who have always encouraged me to write and follow my dreams. I am thankful for their willingness to step out with me in the adventures and unknowns that are always ahead.

I am just as grateful for you, the reader. Thank you for picking up this book. My prayer is that this *AWAKE: 40 Days of Prayer* devotional blesses you and draws you into a closer relationship with Jesus Christ. I also pray that you will pass this book and/or our website on to someone who you think can benefit from this forty days with the Lord.

Foreword by the Author

I am writing this devotional in the midst of the Coronavirus pandemic affecting the entire world. People are living in fear of the unknown and are isolating themselves, afraid to even walk outside for fear of getting or spreading the virus. As the lead pastor of a church, trying my very best to please the Lord more than people, this truly is a challenging time.

During this pandemic I have wondered many times, "What does pastoring a church truly look like in the future?" I have come to realize through my own spiritual journey, ministry, and overall struggles, how I have fallen short and have recognized my great need for the Lord. I have realized how spiritually unprepared the church is and how much we need to wake up and let Christ shine through us. I say this not to condemn you, the Church, or even me, but to wake us up during these next 40 days of prayer, not just for our nation or this world, but also for us to get right with the Lord. Allow Jesus to awaken you, and let Him shine in you and through you.

The purpose of this devotional booklet is for us to be spiritually awake, to let Christ shine in us and to stand firm in our faith. Recently, I have heard of and have had friends pass in tragic ways: boating accidents, car accidents, and a skateboarding accident. They were here one day and gone the next, and I am always reminded that we are not promised tomorrow. Therefore, we must always be spiritually ready, no matter when the Lord calls us home.

In Mark 13:32, we are reminded that no one knows the day or hour Christ will return, not the angels or the Son, but only the Father. Then in verse 33, we get a clear warning, "Be on guard! Be alert! You do not know when that time will come." The most important lesson from this passage is that we need to be spiritually prepared.

My team and I made this booklet very generic in nature so it can be used at any time. Please feel free to pass it on to others. Allow each day's reading to awaken your soul and help you become spiritually ready for whatever comes.

Nate Kingsbury

Awake
BEFORE YOU BEGIN

Preparing Your Heart

Relax. Stop and focus. I have found that during our time with the Lord is when Satan hits us the hardest.

Here are a few ways you can prepare to study the Lord's Word:

Ask the Lord to quiet your mind and heart as you begin.

Take a piece of paper and write down anything that you have to get done later in the day or tomorrow. If you don't take the time to do this before you start, then thinking about your schedule will distract you from what the Lord wants to teach you.

Use your resources. Grab your Bible, listen to podcasts, write in a journal, or whatever will help you in your time with the Lord.

Be you. Talk with the Lord like He is a trusted friend.

Get comfortable. Find a place where you can sit and relax with no distractions. Be aware that it will be easy to fall asleep, so maybe have something to drink to help you stay focused.

Wait on the Lord. Listen for the Lord and what He wants you to hear from Him today.

Put your iPhone in the other room, or just turn it off for a while. Focus on the Lord with nothing distracting you.

Pray against Satan, demons, and their distractions. Satan hates it when we spend time focusing on the Lord. Part of the reason time with the Lord is so difficult is because the forces of darkness do everything to stop and distract us.

Preparation time doesn't have to be long; in fact, it could be only a few minutes. The important part is beginning to relax ourselves in order to focus on hearing from the Lord.

Fasting

In the Bible we read that Jesus would get away to solitary places, away from people or any distractions, to pray to his Father (Mark 1:35; Matthew 6:6). We also read that Jesus would get away to fast and pray, and that this exercise of fasting was done in secret and not meant to be seen, but actually unseen. Fasting is between you and the Lord.

What is Fasting?
Fasting means to refrain from food and drink for a certain period of time. It is designed to humble us and draw us closer to God. Fasting is giving up something of value to focus our attention on the Lord and to replace that desire with spending time focusing on the Lord.

During your time of fasting, God could reveal his true direction for your life. He could reveal an area in your life that needs to be cleaned up. He could awaken you spiritually in ways you didn't think could be possible. He may want to strengthen you spiritually for hard times that may be ahead. He may want to move in you and begin to draw you to a closer relationship with Him. We have to be willing to allow the Lord to work in us and through us.

My hope is that God will reveal to you something that you could fast from for the next 40 days while you dive into this book. Here are a few examples of ways to fast.

Fast from:
-your phone and/or television
-gaming or social media
-one meal each day
-candy and/or soda
-watching sports games
-or give up your weekly Friday afternoon golf

What is God revealing to you from the examples above, or what has he placed on your heart to give up, so you can truly focus on what the Lord wants to teach you in the next forty days? Write it down on a piece of paper or in your journal, and put it somewhere to remind you.

Reflect, Listen, and Write

Many people have Apple products. They have an iPhone, Apple Watch, a computer, iPad, and even AirPods. All of these products have the ability to sync up with one another. You can see your calendar, notes, receive a call, a text message, or listen to your music on all your devices. I desire for you to sync up with the Lord in these next forty days. Below are a few questions for you to ponder before you start this devotional.

Take some time to stop, be still, and just listen. Write down what the Lord is is showing you before you start this forty days of prayer devotional.

In what ways have you gotten out of sync in your relationship with the Lord, and what is being revealed to you right now?

What is God showing to you that needs to get reset in your life so you can take full advantage of this experience?

What do you hope you will look like after this experience?

Section

1

PRAYER & GROWTH

The six sections
of each day's devotional

Scripture
Meditate on the truth from the Bible.

Thought
A small devotional thought to prepare your heart before you pray.

Be honest
Question(s) to make you think and reflect on what you just read.

Ways to pray
Prayer ideas to help you seek the Lord.

Prayer
A written prayer to assist you in praying.

Today's Next Step
An action step that assists you in putting your faith into action. Trust me, if you do this action step, you will see the Lord move in powerful ways.

Day 1
Wake Up, Sleeper!

Ephesians 5:14-16
This is why it is said: "Wake up, sleeper, rise from the dead, and Christ will shine on you." Be very careful, then, how you live—not as unwise but as wise, making the most of every opportunity, because the days are evil.

We must wake up and rise from our spiritual blindness. We must open our eyes to the signs of the times we are living in. I am not saying we are in the end times, but I do believe that we need to wake up to what is going on in our world. We must let Christ shine in us, allowing the presence of the Holy Spirit and the power of the Word of God to transform our lives. We must live carefully, be wise, and make the most of the opportunities the Lord gives us, because these days are evil. We must let our light shine in the darkness. We have an opportunity before us to share about Jesus, to pray for those who are hurting, engage in discussion, and bring hope to those who are fearful. Remember, the first thing we must do is wake up and allow Jesus to shine in us and through us. Allow the Lord to wake you up spiritually and to begin to do a fresh work in your life spiritually. This new journey of being awake starts today. Don't miss the opportunities to allow the Lord to radically change you and awaken you spiritually for the work he wants to do in and through you.

Be honest
Are you awake or are you asleep spiritually?

Ways to pray
1. Ask the Lord to wake you up spiritually.
2. Ask Jesus Christ to shine through you.
3. Ask the Holy Spirit to help you make the most of every opportunity.

Dear Lord,
I ask You to spiritually awaken me individually, and the Church as a whole. Help those who are sleeping to rise up and be spiritually prepared. Help each of us to allow your Holy Spirit to work in us and through us, and the Word to transform us to be more like You. Help us to be careful, to be wise, and to not miss the opportunities that You place before us.
In the name of Jesus, Amen.

Today's Next Step
Go into the bathroom, turn on the faucet, run cold water, and splash it on your face. Let it be a reminder to you every time you wash your face or take a shower to wake up for what the Lord wants to do in you and through you.

Day 2

Hell Is For Real

Revelation 20:11-12; 15
Then I saw a great white throne and him who was seated on it. The earth and the heavens fled from his presence, and there was no place for them. And I saw the dead, great and small, standing before the throne, and books were opened. Another book was opened, which is the book of life. The dead were judged according to what they had done as recorded in the books... Anyone whose name was not found written in the book of life was thrown into the lake of fire.

I have found over the years that there are many different views of hell. Some believe there are different stages of hell like in Dantes' Inferno. Some believe in hell, and I have found recently that others do not. I have heard people say the Lord is too loving and gracious to ever let someone go to hell. I have heard people say we experience hell all the time (broken relationship, death, etc) on this earth. Therefore, there is no hell, because the Lord is too loving. I believe what 2 Timothy 3:16-17 states: "All Scripture is the Lord-breathed and is useful for teaching, rebuking, correcting and training in righteousness, so that the servant of the Lord may be thoroughly equipped for every good work." The Bible says hell is a place of everlasting burning (Isaiah 33:14). It's a fire that does not go out, the pain never stops, there is a lack of peace, and a constant fear that is unending.

Jude 1:13 tells us hell is an isolated torment, a place of darkness forever, a place from which we can never get away. It is everlasting separation from the Lord's presence (2 Thessalonians 1:8-9). Remember that Jesus waits patiently for us, and in His loving kindness He brings us to repentance. He does not want us to go to hell and we have an opportunity to ask Jesus to be the Lord and Savior of our lives.

Be honest
When was the last time you truly had a discussion about sin and hell?

Ways to pray
1. Evaluate and make sure your relationship with Jesus Christ is on point.
2. Ask the Lord to spiritually prepare you for the evil that is ahead.
3. Ask the Lord to turn you back toward the things of the Lord.

Dear Lord,
Help me take the concept of hell and sin seriously today. Help me to understand that I will stand before You someday and help me to not be afraid, but be confident because I know You, Jesus, are my savior. Thank you for forgiving me.
In the name of Jesus, Amen.

Today's Next Step
Spend time looking through the Bible to see what it says about heaven and hell.

Ephesians 6:10-12
Finally, be strong in the Lord and in his mighty power. Put on the full armor of the Lord, so that you can take your stand against the devil's schemes. For our struggle is not against flesh and blood, but against the rulers, against the authorities, against the powers of this dark world and against the spiritual forces of evil in the heavenly realms.

We must understand that we are in a spiritual battle. There is a war going on in the spiritual realm. We must understand who we are fighting. We must be alert, with our eyes wide open. We must put on the full armor of the Lord and be strong in the Lord. We must stand firm against all the tricks of the evil one. Please understand you are not fighting alone. You have Jesus. He conquered the grave, and He defeated the devil already. Remember, in the end we win. The devil is a bitter enemy against the Lord and His people. The devil wants complete power and control, and he is over the powers of darkness. He has the power behind the world's system, and he is working through leaders, music, news stations, and anyone who lives in disobedience. Please understand that he came from Heaven (Ezekiel 28:14) and wanted the power (Isaiah 14:13-14). Satan was kicked out of Heaven and became a fallen angel (Ezekiel 28:16-17). His mission is to kill, steal and destroy, and he wants nothing more than to hurt Christ-followers, mess up families, and destroy the Church. We must put on the Lord's armor, and be prepared for the battle that is ahead.

Be honest
How do you see the devil currently working in the United States?

Ways to pray
1. Ask the Lord to give you strength to withstand the attacks of the evil one.
2. Ask the Lord to help you be alert and aware of who the enemy is and how he is working within you and your family.
3. Ask the Lord to protect you and your family, and send His angel armies to guard you.

Dear Lord,
Help me to recognize the enemy and understand that I am currently in a spiritual battle. Help me to not be deceived, but to see clearly what is going on. Protect me and my family. Help me to be fully equipped with spiritual armor, and to be ready to fight.
In the name of Jesus, Amen.

Today's Next Step
Look up Ephesians 6:10-18. Copy that passage, and tape it to your bathroom mirror. Commit to reading that passage daily, and then do so.

Day 4

Be Anchored

Hebrews 6:19
We have this hope as an anchor for the soul, firm and secure.

People are looking for hope. We try to find hope in many different ways. We search for it in relationships, in money, in success, and in friendships. We look for the approval of others. We will never find true hope in the treasures of this world; we must find our hope in Jesus Christ. For many of us, Jesus Christ is not our anchor. Something else may have taken His place. If you lost your home, if your company got downsized, if you lost the most important person in your life, if it was all gone, what would you have left? Many of us find our anchor in our Christian community. We may rely on our Sunday School class, or our small group, to feed us spiritually. Many times I used church camp to get myself spiritually fit, or I would rely on my parents' faith instead of finding my hope in Jesus Christ. Many times we rely on our pastor to give us our spiritual food for the week or the worship pastor to bring us to the Lord's throne room. Your relationship can't be based on a pastor, a church camp, or a worship experience. Your relationship can't be based on a feeling or an emotional experience. Your anchor must be Jesus. Is Jesus enough? Is He your anchor?

Be honest
Who or what do you truly rely on as your anchor?

Ways to pray
1. Admit and confess to the Lord the people or things you have placed over Him.
2. Seek forgiveness from the Lord and repent of any sin that has control over you.
3. Establish Jesus as your anchor.

Dear Lord,
I have come to realize that my hope and my attention have not been focused on You. I admit my lack of focus, and I ask for Your forgiveness. I repent of my sins of selfishness and putting possessions and others above You, Lord. I ask You to regain all of my life, and I choose to completely surrender to Your will, Jesus. I desire my anchor to be securely in You.
In the name of Jesus, Amen.

Today's Next Step
If you looked to Jesus as your Savior today, have re-committed your life to the Lord, or even if God is speaking to you in a completely different way, I ask you to be bold by telling two people today on the phone or in-person about what Jesus Christ just did in your life.

Day 5
Solid Foundation

Matthew 7:24-25
Therefore everyone who hears these words of mine and puts them into practice is like a wise man who built his house on the rock. The rain came down, the streams rose, and the winds blew and beat against that house; yet it did not fall, because it had its foundation on the rock.

At the age of seven, I gave my life to Jesus. At age 14, I felt called to be a pastor. I went to college when I was 19 and studied to be a pastor. My junior year of college, I lost a friend to the effects of alcohol. This event shook me greatly, and I questioned my faith and my calling to be a pastor. I went through deep sadness. I locked myself in my dorm room, my grades dropped, and I didn't want to move. During this time, I realized my foundation was not built on the Lord, but on my parents' faith. They built a great foundation in me, but it was not my own. I questioned if I even knew Jesus as my Savior. My relationship was built on emotion, my parents' faith, and my camp experiences, but I was not grounded in Christ. I was even studying for ministry, but I was lost. It took a crisis for me to truly realize that I was blinded and that I needed Jesus Christ. Are you building your relationship on bedrock? When storms come and flood waters rise, will your house stand? No matter if you are a new Christ-follower or you consider yourself a seasoned Christ-follower, if you are not built on Christ, you will crash.

Be honest
Upon what kind of foundation is your relationship with Jesus Christ built? In what way do you feel your foundation could be stronger?

Ways to pray
1. Ask the Lord to reveal what kind of foundation you are currently building.
2. Ask the Lord to give you attentive ears to listen and obey His teachings.
3. Ask the Lord to strengthen your relationship with Him.

Dear Lord,
Help me and my family to build our foundation on Your bedrock. Help me be so secure in You that when the winds and waves hit against my foundation, I won't be moved. Thank you Jesus for saving me and giving me confidence in You.
In the name of Jesus, Amen.

Today's Next Step
Go find a rock and put it somewhere that you will see it to remind you to have a firm foundation.

Day 6

Road Map

2 Timothy 3:16-17
All Scripture is the Lord-breathed and is useful for teaching, rebuking, correcting and training in righteousness, so that the servant of the Lord may be thoroughly equipped for every good work.

I believe the Word of God, the Bible, is a map to help guide us in our relationship with the Lord. It's a love letter given to us by the Lord. The Word produces lasting fruit in our lives that helps us grow to be more like Jesus, and the Word is a weapon used to fight the forces of evil. The Bible is the inspired Word of God, and it is used to train us in righteousness. It consists of 66 books with 40 different authors. The writing of the Bible took over 1000 years, and it is still the best-selling book of all time. Psalm 119:105 says, "Your Word is a lamp for my feet, a light on my path." The Bible reveals to us who God is, what his plan is for our lives, and helps us to experience a closer relationship with Jesus Christ. The Bible teaches us what is true. The Word thoroughly equips us for every good work he has for us to do. Don't miss any opportunity to spend time in the Word and allow the Lord to convict, encourage, challenge, equip, and give you wisdom.

Be honest
When was the last time you truly read the Word of the Lord, took the truth learned, and applied it to your life?

Ways to pray
1. Ask the Lord to give you the desire to read His Word and seek His direction in your life.
2. Ask the Holy Spirit to reveal to you what is right and what is wrong in your life, based on what you are reading in the Word.
3. Ask the Lord to allow the Word to teach, rebuke, correct, prepare and equip you for the work He has for you.

Dear Lord,
Remind me that Your Word is inspired by You, and that it teaches me what is right and what is wrong in my life. Let Your Word correct my wrongs and teach me what is right. Lord, prepare me spiritually and equip me for the work You are calling me to do.
In the name of Jesus, Amen.

Today's Next Step
Pull out your cell phone, pick a time daily, make an appointment with the Lord, and do not let anything interfere with your time with Jesus.

Hebrews 12:1
Therefore, since we are surrounded by such a great cloud of witnesses, let us throw off everything that hinders and the sin that so easily entangles.

Sometimes we have to be aware of the roadblocks that block the Holy Spirit from moving within our lives. Not being willing to forgive is a roadblock that affects us spiritually. Satan uses unforgiveness to stop the spiritual growth Jesus wants to do in our life. Another hindrance is when we choose not to, or get distracted from, studying the Bible. We must not just listen to the Word of the Lord, but we must do what the Word says. Another issue is a lack of family unity that exists in our homes. This can be a roadblock to our prayers. The Lord wants to heal broken marriages and restore homes that are fractured. When we don't feel close to the Lord, it could be directly connected to our home life. Another huge roadblock to the Lord moving in our lives is unconfessed sin that we have allowed to live inside us. We must allow the Lord to cleanse us from our sin, so that we can experience all that Jesus wants to do in our lives. If we become free of these roadblocks, I believe we will encounter the work of the Holy Spirit even more.

Be honest
With what roadblock or hindrance are you currently struggling?

Ways to pray
1. Forgive anyone whom you may have unforgiveness toward, and allow the Lord to set you free.
2. Ask the Lord to heal your home and/or marriage so that you can hear more clearly from Him.
3. Confess any sin that has been ruling your heart and/or mind.

Dear Lord,
Please help me to forgive those who have wronged me and hold no bitterness toward them. Help me to stay true to Your Word and keep it in my heart in all that I do. Lord, heal and restore any issues that exist in my family. I want nothing to stop You from truly moving in my life. Lord, if there is any darkness that still exists in my life, please shine Your light onto it, so that I can confess it and let it go. Free me from any roadblocks that exist in me. **In the name of Jesus, Amen.**

Today's Next Step
Ask one person you deeply respect to point out the roadblocks that exist in your life that you have been unable to recognize.

We Must Stand

Ephesians 6:13-17

Therefore put on the full armor of the Lord, so that when the day of evil comes, you may be able to stand your ground, and after you have done everything, to stand. Stand firm then, with the belt of truth buckled around your waist, with the breastplate of righteousness in place, and with your feet fitted with the readiness that comes from the gospel of peace. In addition to all this, take up the shield of faith, with which you can extinguish all the flaming arrows of the evil one. Take the helmet of salvation and the sword of the Spirit, which is the word of the Lord.

You must stand up, and remember, you have the full armor of the Lord. Be strong in the Lord and in His power. You have the belt of truth, knowing who you are and who the Lord is through the Bible. Put on the breastplate of righteousness which represents living a holy life. Tie your shoes with the Gospel that has the power to change lives. Use the shield of faith to protect you from Satan's attack. Put on your helmet of salvation which protects your mind, and fight with the sword of the Spirit, which is the Word of the Lord and has the power to destroy the tricks of the evil one. Make a decision to surrender to Jesus daily (2 Corinthians 7:10). Understand that we fight with the power of the Word of the Lord (Hebrews 4:12). Remember to pray in the Spirit on all occasions and stay alert (Ephesians 6:18). Remember there is power in the name of Jesus and even the demons obey (Luke 10:17).

Be honest

In what ways do you believe you are currently in a spiritual battle?

Ways to pray

1. Read through Ephesians 6:10-17, and visualize putting on every piece of the armor of the Lord.
2. Ask the Lord for protection over you, your family, and your church.
3. Ask the Lord to bring you and your family back to your knees, to truly surrender to Him.

Dear Lord,

Help me to put on Your armor daily. Help me to be strong in You and in Your mighty power. Give me the strength to see Satan's attacks and to stand firm against all of his tricks. Give me the boldness to fight for me, my family, my church, and this nation.

In the name of Jesus, Amen.

Today's Next Step

Call up a trusted, spiritual person that the Lord has placed in your life, and ask them if you can pray with them. Have them pray for you for strength and boldness, and you do the same for them.

Day 9

Iron Sharpens Iron

Ecclesiastes 4:9-10
Two are better than one, because they have a good return for their labor. If either of them falls down, one can help the other up. But pity anyone who falls and has no one to help them up.

I believe that every person needs an accountability partner that helps hold them accountable and truly looks out for them spiritually. I also believe that each of us could use a spiritual coach, someone further along in their spiritual walk that can truly push us to a deeper level. Another way for us to be sharpened spiritually that we may not think about is mentoring. We can pour our lives into someone to help them grow in Christ. Accountability is so important. If we fall, we have someone to help us up. In Proverbs 27:17 it says, "As iron sharpens iron, so one person sharpens another." We need godly people around us to sharpen us spiritually, and when we sharpen others, it also sharpens us.

Be honest

Who is your accountability partner? Who is your spiritual coach? Into whom are you pouring your life?

Ways to pray

1. Ask the Lord to reveal a person you can be real and transparent with, someone you respect, that you can ask to be an accountability partner or your spiritual coach.
2. Ask the Lord to reveal a person you could mentor and help to grow in Christ.
3. Ask the Lord to give you a gentle attitude as you deal with people.

Dear Lord,

Please reveal to me a person I can be real with about where I fall short. Bring a person into my life that will encourage me and help me grow in my relationship with You. Help us to truly sharpen one another, and push each other to be more like Jesus. Show me the person You wish me to pour into and mentor in his or her walk with You.
In the name of Jesus, Amen.

Today's Next Step

Write a list of five possible coaches to help you grow, five possible accountability partners, and five possible people you can help grow. Pray over those lists and ask the Lord to reveal who you should ask to be your coach, your accountability partner, and who to mentor.

Hebrews 12:1-2a
Therefore, since we are surrounded by such a great cloud of witnesses, let us throw off everything that hinders and the sin that so easily entangles. And let us run with perseverance the race marked out for us, fixing our eyes on Jesus, the pioneer and perfecter of faith.

We live in a period in our history where anything goes, a "whatever" society. What is right is wrong and what is wrong is right. Sin is so rampant. It is hurting us individually, and it is destroying our nation. We must get our attention focused on Jesus again. Are you focused on the pleasures of this world or are you fixing your eyes on the Lord? The verse above tells us to "throw off everything that hinders" us. Maybe God is revealing to you a friendship, relationship, or bad habit that is hindering your connection with the Lord. The verse also reminds us to get rid of the "sin that so easily entangles" us. When we struggle spiritually, we have a difficult time recognizing our sin or hindrances. We have to wake up, and we must be willing to throw off everything that slows us down and get rid of the sin that weighs us down. Jesus wants to set you free, so decide today to identify these roadblocks, repent of your blind spots, and ask God to forgive you for the sin you have allowed in your life. Choose today to walk in the freedom the Lord wants to give, seek his forgiveness, and "run with perseverance the race marked out for us, fixing our eyes on Jesus."

Be honest
What sin do you need to remove from your life?

Ways to pray
1. Ask the Lord to reveal the sin that is in you, and then ask Him to forgive you.
2. Ask the Lord to reveal any habits or behaviors that are causing you to sin, ask for forgiveness, and then ask Him to help you change those habits.
3. Recognize the Lord as your hope.

Dear Lord,
Help me to recognize my sin. Point out the areas in my life that have to be surrendered. Help me see the sin that is running freely. Please convict and make me aware of wickedness in my life. Please, Lord, begin to bring me back to You. You are my Only Hope.
In the name of Jesus, Amen.

Today's Next Step
Find a person in your life that you trust, and ask them to point out the areas in which you are falling short. Then commit to changing those areas, and begin by picking some intentional next steps.

Matthew 23:28
In the same way, on the outside you appear to people as righteous but on the inside you are full of hypocrisy and wickedness.

I believe there are four types of masks that everyone puts on at some point in their life. The first is the "cool" mask. We act like everything is okay, when it really is not. The second is a "clown" mask. We act as if we are the life of the party, when we are really hurting or sad. The third is a "silent" mask. We choose to keep everything inside, even though we want to explode. The last is a "Christian" mask. We act as if we have it all together spiritually, when we are feeling dead or dry in our walk with the Lord. Each of these masks represent the majority of the population, and I believe we all wear at least one of these masks, hiding who we really are. Many times people wear these masks because they don't like who they are, or desire to be like someone else. In the passage above, Jesus was talking about the Pharisees and how they are like white-washed tombs who look beautiful on the outside, but on the inside are just dead bones. Everyone can find freedom from their pain and be the person that the Lord intended them to be, their true self, when they choose to take off their identity masks.

Be honest
What identity mask are you currently wearing?

Ways to pray
1. Ask the Lord to help you remove the identity mask(s) you are currently wearing and be your true self.
2. Ask the Lord to show you the lies and deception around you, and then fill you with the truth to set you free.
3. Ask the Lord to humble you enough to admit your own mistakes, and to be willing to show mercy and grace when someone fails.

Dear Lord,
Help me to stop hiding in my pain, behind false identities, and to be transparent about my struggles. Please set me free. If I have any hypocrisy in me, please reveal it to me, and help me to begin to walk in truth.
In the name of Jesus, Amen.

Today's Next Step
Grab a piece of paper and write down the identity mask that you are wearing. Grab that paper, go to your backyard, and burn it. Remind yourself that you will not hide behind that identity mask again.

Day 12

Renewed Mind

Romans 12:2
Do not conform to the pattern of this world, but be transformed by the renewing of your mind. Then you will be able to test and approve what the Lord's will is—his good, pleasing and perfect will.

This Bible verse tells us to not be like the world, but renew our minds with the things of the Lord. The Holy Spirit is like a floodlight, exposing things in our lives that need to be seen. As the Holy Spirit gains control, we gain a brand new perspective on sin. He brings out more things that we need to turn over to Him. We begin to no longer watch the shows we used to watch, we decide to no longer hang out with the friends we used to hang out with, we can no longer be dishonest, and we begin to recognize the nagging thoughts that come from the devil. Our minds are being renewed by the Holy Spirit. We are being transformed by Him, making our thoughts obedient to the Lord and allowing the Holy Spirit to work in us. In the midst of living in this fear-based world, we need to start a new way of thinking and begin to trust in the Lord, gaining spiritual muscle and a way of thinking that gives us joy in the midst of these storms.

Be honest
On what is your mind currently focused?

Ways to pray
1. Ask the Lord to reveal to you the ways that you are conforming to the patterns of this world.
2. Ask the Lord to transform your mind and make you more like Jesus.
3. Ask the Lord to give you wisdom to know what His good, pleasing and perfect will is for your life.

Dear Lord,
I renew my mind, and I fix my eyes on You. I will take every thought captive and make it obedient to You. I will not conform to this world and its temptations, but I will be transformed by You. Use my mind, change it, and transform it.
In the name of Jesus, Amen.

Today's Next Step
Every time a negative thought bounces into your brain, renew your mind and give that thought right over to Jesus. In fact, I encourage you to do it right now.

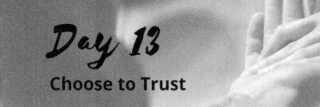

Day 13

Choose to Trust

Proverbs 3:5-6
Trust in the Lord with all your heart and lean not on your own understanding; in all your ways submit to him, and he will make your paths straight.

Each of us trust a chair to hold our weight. We trust a vehicle to get us safely to our destination. We trust pilots to fly us across an ocean in a jet with our family members. If we can put our trust in a chair, an automobile, or a pilot, then why can't we put our trust in Jesus? It's so easy to sit in the chair or drive our vehicle, but we can't seem to trust the Lord in times of uncertainty. We must lean on His understanding and trust in Him. Every morning when you wake up, choose to trust in Jesus, submit to Him, and lean on His understanding.

Be honest
Are you trusting in the Lord, or are you living in fear of the world's uncertainties?

Ways to pray
1. Ask the Lord to take away any fear, worry, and anxiety that exists in you.
2. Ask the Lord to point out areas where you are leaning on your own understanding and not His.
3. Ask the Lord to help you trust Him, and submit yourself to Him.

Dear Lord,
Help me to truly learn to trust You. Help me to not lean on my own understanding, but help me to truly submit to You and cast my concerns and worries at Your feet, Jesus. Give me peace, confidence, and courage to completely trust in You.
In the name of Jesus, Amen.

Today's Next Step
Memorize Proverbs 3:5-6. Make a decision daily to trust in the Lord, and lean on His understanding. Make a sign to hang on your wall to look at every day.

Luke 12:25
Who of you by worrying can add a single hour to his life?

Many Christ-followers worry instead of giving their worry over to the Lord. Will my parents get divorced? Is my marriage going to make it? Will the Lord heal the brokenness in my family? Guys ask, "Do I have what it takes to succeed?" Girls ask, "Am I pretty enough?" The older generation asks, "Will I get sick?" and "What does my future hold?" It seems like we live in a culture of worry. We have to find a way to stop the worry that exists in our lives. I believe that the Lord can lessen, and for some people completely release, the worry that exists in our lives. You see, worry causes more stress in your life than actually helping you succeed. It makes things worse. Worry is bad for your health. In fact, the word "worry" literally means to strangle, constrict, or choke the life out of you. I have to do everything I can to stop worry in my life, so I don't pass it down to my children.

Be honest
What are you currently worried about? How is your worry actually hindering you?

Ways to pray
1. Spend time thanking the Lord for how great He is.
2. Turn on praise and worship music and sing praises to the Lord, allowing yourself to forget the worries and to trust in Him.
3. Whenever you start to worry, stop and give your worries to the Lord.

Dear Lord,
Free me from the worry and burdens of this life. Help me to not let life circumstances affect me. I choose to not worry about anything. I put my trust in You. Help me to no longer allow stress to strangle me, but help me to truly worship and praise Your name when worry arrives. Help me to always be reminded that worry does not add a single hour to my life.
In the name of Jesus, Amen.

Today's Next Step
When you start to worry, write that worry on a piece of paper. Read the worry out loud. Many times as you read it, you will realize that what you wrote down is not worth worrying about any longer. Then give it to Jesus.

Hebrews 12:1-2
Let us run with perseverance the race marked out for us, fixing our eyes on Jesus, the pioneer and perfecter of faith. For the joy set before him he endured the cross, scorning its shame, and sat down at the right hand of the throne of God.

When you drive, if you spend too much time looking in the rearview mirror, you could get into an accident. If you spend so much time focused on looking back at how bad your job is, you can't see how good it really is. In your marriage, if all you see is an obstacle, you won't be able to see the opportunity. If all you see is our nation's struggles, you will be blinded to the way the Lord could be moving. Quit looking backwards, stop complaining and allowing fear to control you. Take your eyes off the circumstances that are around you and focus your eyes on the Lord. Don't look back; keep your eyes looking forward, focusing on Jesus Christ. The devil loves to see us frozen in fear, focusing on our past and the mess that is around us, but the Lord desires for us to fix our eyes on Him. Anything that takes your attention away from your relationship with Jesus Christ is stealing your focus. The devil loves to use our iPhone, work, social media, and even our hobbies to get our focus off Jesus. The devil is also using fear to cripple us. Be aware! Open your eyes, and be aware of his tricks and do something about it today.

Be honest
What currently has the attention in your life?

Ways to pray
1. Admit where your focus has been lately.
2. Confess any ways you have been focusing on the past and living in fear.
3. Ask the Lord to help you fix your eyes back on Him.

Dear Lord,
Help me to fix my eyes on You, Jesus. Help me love You with all my heart, mind, soul and strength. Help me to truly put others above myself. Help me to not focus on the pleasures of this world, but to fix my eyes on You, Your word and Your perfect plan. Help me be so close to You that I hear Your voice and walk in step with the Holy Spirit.
In the name of Jesus, Amen.

Today's Next Step
Write out a 3-5 step plan of practical ways to keep your eyes on Jesus. Share this plan with a spiritual mentor you respect.

1 Peter 1:14-16
As obedient children, do not conform to the evil desires you had when you lived in ignorance. But just as he who called you is holy, so be holy in all you do; for it is written: "Be holy, because I am holy."

The disciples watched Jesus perform many miracles. They saw how He confronted sin and stood up against the Pharisees and religious leaders, calling them out for their hypocrisy. They witnessed the way Jesus cared for those who were hurt and how He allowed children to be a part of His life. They witnessed Jesus despising sin, and they saw how He was able to resist temptation from the evil one. They saw Jesus' commitment to get away in solitude and pray to His father. The disciples modeled their lives after Jesus. They slept near each other, they laughed, they cried, and they fought evil together on a daily basis. They saw holiness and were given the greatest example to follow. As we read the Bible, we must learn from the disciples, letting Jesus influence us and our church. We used to live in sin, but Jesus has called us to be holy. This means we are to be careful how we talk, what we laugh at, which programs we watch, with whom we hang out, and that our outsides match our insides. We imitate the Lord in everything we do and follow His example. This seems impossible, but the more we follow and love the Lord it becomes possible, because Jesus lives in us.

Be honest
In what ways are you being holy in all you do?

Ways to pray
1. Ask the Lord to show you how you can be more like Him in all that you do.
2. Ask the Lord to produce a deep passion in you to truly love Him more than you ever have before.
3. Ask the Lord for wisdom to live like Him in each step of your life.

Dear Lord,
Help me to discern what is right and what is wrong, and act rightly. Help me be so close to You, Jesus, that I can actually hear Your directions to me. Help me imitate You in all I do, to be different from this world, and set apart for the work You have called me to do.
In the name of Jesus, Amen.

Today's Next Step
Write down three practical ways you can truly begin to imitate the Lord in all you do, and start right away. Ask God to reveal to you someone with whom you could share these practical things.

John 1:5
The light shines in the darkness, and the darkness has not overcome it.

Many times, as Christ-followers, we run from the darkness. We are scared of what we may see or find. Many years back, I was taught to stay away from the darkness because it would destroy me or my ministry. Because of this idea, I would stay away from dangers even though my heart was burdened for those who were hurting. I felt like the light of Christ in me could help people struggling in darkness. People live in fear and now is our chance to be the light of Christ. As Christians, we can't ignore the darkness. We must take our light (Christ) into dangerous territories. Our light shines brighter in the darkness. Don't be afraid. Go into the darkness shining the light of Christ. Let's help bring people out of their darkness and into the freedom that is offered by Jesus. Let your light shine in this time of darkness.

Be honest
In what ways are you running from darkness? In what ways can you bring the light of Christ into that darkness?

Ways to pray
1. Ask the Holy Spirit to use the light of Christ to illuminate your darkness.
2. Ask the Lord for boldness and to reveal what darkness you need to run toward.
3. Ask the Lord to turn our nation away from darkness and to fix our eyes on Him.

Dear Lord,
Reveal to me any darkness in me, illuminate that darkness, and fill me with Your light, Jesus. Give me boldness to walk into darkness with no fear, but with Your power, strength, and complete protection.
In the name of Jesus, Amen.

Today's Next Step
Write down the darkness the Lord is asking you to run toward, and pray to God about your plan to go into that darkness. Then go and do it.

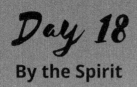

Day 18

By the Spirit

Galatians 5:25
Since we live by the Spirit, let us keep in step with the Spirit.

The Holy Spirit is the Lord's agent on earth, yet it's the least-discussed member of the Trinity. Without the Holy Spirit, our spiritual lives become stagnant. When the Holy Spirit moves in us, our prayer life deepens, the Word of the Lord comes alive, we experience worship in a different way, and we find deep joy in the Lord. We develop a passion to tell people about Jesus, and the Spirit of the Lord joins us in a fresh and new way. The Holy Spirit is our Counselor guiding us, helping us, and comforting us. The Holy Spirit is like a GPS built into our chest that tells us what is right and what is wrong. He tells us when we are in danger or when we are safe. Take a moment every day to be silent, be still, and listen intently to what the Lord may be revealing in your life. Grab a notepad and write down what the Holy Spirit is revealing to you. In that very moment, don't hesitate, but do exactly what the Holy Spirit revealed. Be aware of the way He begins to move in your life.

Be honest

In what ways are you currently seeing the Holy Spirit work in your life?

Ways to pray

1. Ask the Holy Spirit to start working and moving in your life immediately, and on a daily basis.
2. Ask the Lord to help you be a source of wisdom for other believers.
3. Ask the Lord to help you put your preferences, agenda and style aside, allowing Him to move freely.

Dear Lord,

Help me to listen to You and be able to recognize Your voice. Show me who I need to pray for, and lead me to the people I need to encourage. Convict me when I start to gossip and when sin is creeping into my life. Help me to listen to You when You tell me to apologize and give me the boldness when I need to confront others. Reveal opportunities to spread the gospel. Help me walk as close to You as I can. Be my Guide, my Helper, and my Counselor. **In the name of Jesus, Amen.**

Today's Next Step

Wake up tomorrow morning and say, "Holy Spirit, give me an opportunity today to encourage, to bring joy to someone who needs it, or to pray for someone who is fearful. Help me to not miss the moments You place before me. I will be watching today for Your opportunities."

Luke 1:13
But the angel said to him: "Do not be afraid, Zechariah; your prayer has been heard. Your wife Elizabeth will bear you a son, and you are to call him John."

Sometimes the Lord wants to do the impossible. Zechariah and Elizabeth were too old to have kids, but the Lord did the impossible by giving them a son. When I look at all that is going on in our culture, it is obvious that we don't believe the Lord can truly bring a miracle to the situations we are facing. I want to remind you that nothing is impossible for the Lord. I am praying for the Lord to truly perform a miracle and unite our country. I am praying He will take away fear. We must remember that the Lord can answer the impossible prayer (Matthew 19:26). We need to understand that the Lord hears the prayers of the righteous. We also must realize that impossible things happen when we believe in the Lord's power. For many years people have prayed to be healed from cancer. Parents have asked me to pray that their child would come back to Jesus again. Others have asked for the Lord to get their children out of the legal problems they are facing. Each of us has an impossible prayer request, and I believe that the Lord wants to answer the impossible.

Be honest
What is the impossible request that you want the Lord to answer?

Ways to pray
1. Ask the Lord to answer your impossible request.
2. Ask the Lord to give you faith that He will perform miracles in your life.
3. Ask the Lord to reveal to you the miracles He has already done in your life.

Dear Lord,
I give You my impossible. Please give me the faith to know that You are performing miracles in my life. Show me the miracles You have already done, and help me see the miracles You will continue to perform in my life.
In the name of Jesus, Amen.

Today's Next Step
Start a text group with 3-5 prayer warriors that you respect. Ask them if they will be your prayer team and if you can send them a few prayer requests weekly.

Day 20

Individual Revival

Psalms 51:10-13
Create in me a pure heart, O God, and renew a steadfast spirit within me. Do not cast me from your presence or take your Holy Spirit from me. Restore to me the joy of your salvation and grant me a willing spirit, to sustain me. Then I will teach transgressors your ways, so that sinners will turn back to you.

I remember when I was in college, the Holy Spirit showed up in a powerful way in our chapel services and people started confessing sin and were praying all over the college campus. I remember kids were getting up at 6:00 a.m. to pray with our university chaplain, and regular classes were turning into amazing times where professors and students were studying the Bible. After one month of the most amazing spiritual moments that I have ever seen, the revival just stopped. I remember sitting in our student cafe and talking with my friend Cari and she said something that I will never forget as long as I live. She said, "In order for a revival to truly happen on our campus, it has to individually start in us first." We can be a part of a big movement and see the Lord work, but it has to start in us first.

Be honest
How passionate and dedicated are you to Jesus right now in your life?

Ways to pray
1. Ask the Lord to give you a steadfast, unshakeable commitment to Him.
2. Ask the Holy Spirit to move and speak freely in your life.
3. Ask the Lord to allow times of turmoil to bring you back to Him.

Dear Lord,
Help me to truly surrender to You, Jesus. Help my commitment to You to be unshakable during these days in which I am living. Give me a passion for Your Word and increase my prayer life and boldness for You, Jesus. Give me Your wisdom. Help me to hear Your voice and to walk closely to You.
In the name of Jesus, Amen.

Today's Next Step
Google amazing movements of the Lord or revivals in history. Write down why you believe that those great movements happened. Now write down how revival is happening in you.

Section

2

PRAYER & ACTION

The Fellowship of the Unashamed
(An Unknown Rwandan Christian)

I am part of the "Fellowship of the Unashamed." The die has been cast. I have stepped over the line. The decision has been made. I am a disciple of Jesus Christ. I won't look back, let up, slow down, back away, or be still. My past is redeemed, my present makes sense, and my future is secure. I am finished and done with low living, sight walking, small planning, smooth knees, colorless dreams, chintzy giving, and dwarfed goals.

I no longer need pre-eminence, prosperity, position, promotions, plaudits, or popularity. I now live by presence, lean by faith, love by patience, lift by prayer, and labor by power. My pace is set, my gait is fast, my goal is Heaven, my road is narrow, my way is rough, my companions few, my Guide reliable, my mission clear. I cannot be bought, compromised, deterred, lured away, turned back, diluted, or delayed.

I will not flinch in the face of sacrifice, hesitate in the presence of adversity, negotiate at the table of the enemy, ponder at the pool of popularity, or meander in the maze of mediocrity.

I am a disciple of Jesus Christ. I must go until Heaven returns, give until I drop, preach until all know, and work until He comes. And when He comes to get His own, He will have no problem recognizing me. My colors will be clear.

Do You Notice?

Matthew 11:5
The blind receive sight, the lame walk, those who have leprosy are cleansed, the deaf hear, the dead are raised, and the good news is proclaimed to the poor.

The Lord has called us to care for the poor and to bring the hope of the good news of Jesus Christ to the hurting. So many times we ignore the poor that are right before us. A person on the corner holding a sign, a kid living on the streets selling drugs, a mom trying her best to take care of her children doing anything to survive, even a family living in a big house with no furniture trying to act as if they are wealthy. The poor are all around us, but do you notice and do you care? When was the last time you helped a person who is homeless? I am not talking about giving them money, but actually being willing to find out their stories, learning from them, and allowing them to pray for you. We think we are here to help the poor, but in reality we find out that they often impact us more than we do them.

Be honest
When was the last time you connected with someone in need and truly learned their story?

Ways to pray
1. Ask the Lord to give you the boldness to share the good news with the poor.
2. Ask the Lord to help you hear the cries of the poor, and to not ignore them.
3. Ask the Holy Spirit to prompt you to respond the next time you see someone in need, and ask for the courage to interact with that person.

Dear Lord,
I ask You to send me or other believers as messengers to bring the hope of the gospel into the places most of us would never go. Help me to not ignore the cries of the poor, but give me the courage to get into their lives. Please, Lord, give us courage to share the gospel.
In the name of Jesus, Amen.

Today's Next Step
Get online today and find a ministry opportunity near you for you and your family to help the poor. Sign up for it and commit to helping.

Genesis 45:5-7
And now, do not be distressed and do not be angry with yourselves for selling me here, because it was to save lives that God sent me ahead of you. For two years now there has been famine in the land, and for the next five years there will be no plowing and reaping. But God sent me ahead of you to preserve for you a remnant on earth and to save your lives by a great deliverance.

In Genesis we see the story of Joseph and the injustice towards him. His father adored him and his brothers were jealous of him, both because of their father's attention and the dreams that the Lord sent to Joseph. His brothers' jealousy turned to hatred, and they mistreated Joseph. They sold him into slavery and lied to their father, claiming Joseph was dead. Joseph was given an opportunity to run Potiphar's household in Egypt, but was wrongfully accused and put in prison. Joseph spent time there until an opportunity arose for him to interpret a dream for the king. He then became second-in-command of all of Egypt. This story includes the topics of slavery, abandonment, abuse, false accusations, prison time, opportunities, forgiveness, and reconciliation. There is so much for us to learn from Joseph's life. The Lord redeemed a horrible situation, and we see forgiveness and beautiful reconciliation.

Be honest

Have you ever experienced or seen injustice done to those close to you? Have you stood up or spoken up and defended that injustice done to you or others?

Ways to pray

1. Ask the Lord to heal those who have been damaged by injustice, and to help them forgive those who have hurt them.
2. Ask the Lord to grant boldness to those who see injustice, so they stand up against it.
3. Ask the Lord to reveal to you the ways that you have been a part of injustice, and to break your heart for the injustices that you see going on around you.

Dear Lord,

I ask You to convict me of any ways I have been a part of or witnessed injustice and just sat there silently. Lord, I ask You to make me a voice for those who are hurting, and I pray for forgiveness and reconciliation to happen for us and for this nation. Please bring healing to individuals and to this nation.
In the name of Jesus, Amen.

Today's Next Step

Ask the Lord to reveal to you a moment where you could have handled a situation better, and ask the Lord to forgive you right now. Take the steps to ask for forgiveness of that person or people, and to apologize for the way you acted.

Job 1:20-21
At this, Job got up and tore his robe and shaved his head. Then he fell to the ground in worship and said: "Naked I came from my mother's womb, and naked I will depart. The Lord gave and the Lord has taken away; may the name of the Lord be praised."

I remember that as a kid I thought that once I asked Christ into my life all struggles would instantly stop. No more pain, heartache or sadness, right? All of these challenges still exist, but the hope we have in Jesus gives us the strength to endure. Can you imagine the Lord saying these words about you, "There is no one on earth like you; you are blameless and upright. You fear the Lord and you push away evil." Job was anchored in the Lord, but it didn't mean that struggles didn't come his way. Let me break down what happened to him. His oxen and donkeys were stolen and all his servants were killed. Fire fell from the sky and burned up his sheep. His camels were stolen. But here's the stinger: a mighty wind swept in and collapsed his home, and he lost his sons and daughters. Put yourself in Job's shoes. What would you do? You lost all your money, your house, your retirement, your employees were all killed, and then you find out your children are dead. Many would run away from the Lord. Some would run to the Lord. Others would become depressed and stop moving, or live in isolation and never get out.

Some would live in pain and many would not recover. A small number would choose to help others and they would find their strength in the Lord in these tragedies.

Be honest
How do you respond to the Lord in hard circumstances?

Ways to pray
1. Ask the Lord to help you truly understand commitment and love for Him in the midst of suffering.
2. Ask the Lord to strengthen your faith for Him as you face the days ahead.
3. Ask the Lord to use you to bring your friends and family to a closer relationship with Him.

Dear Lord,
Help us as a nation to be anchored like Job, so that we can still stand strong in the midst of suffering. Help us to not just read this story, but allow it to sink in deep, establishing roots in us.
In the name of Jesus, Amen.

Today's Next Step
Spend extra time today looking at the life of Job. Allow the Lord to reveal to you where you can learn from his life. Share with someone else the lessons the Lord has revealed to you in your suffering and in the story of Job.

1 Chronicles 28:20
"Be strong and courageous, and do the work. Do not be afraid or discouraged, for the Lord God, my God, is with you. He will not fail you or forsake you until all the work for the service of the temple of the Lord is finished."

Many people thought it was a tragic waste of a life when Jim Elliot and four other missionaries died trying to contact the unreached Auca Tribe. The last radio contact they made was Jim calling his wife saying, "We'll call you back in three hours." Jim Elliot's body was found downstream with three others. Their bodies had been brutally pierced with spears and hacked by machetes. After Jim's death, his wife, her daughter and one of the other missionaries' sisters moved to work with the Auca Tribe. The love of Christ shown through their forgiveness allowed them to have amazing success with the once murderous tribe members. Jim's life was not a waste. The Lord used his death to bring life through salvation to many Aucas, and encouragement and inspiration to thousands of believers worldwide. How many Christians do you know who would risk their lives for an opportunity to share the gospel? We don't experience persecution like people do in other countries or like the story above, but we see things getting more hostile toward Christians in the United States.

Be honest

In what ways have you experienced persecution in your life? In what ways do you need to step out of your comfort zone?

Ways to pray

1. Ask the Holy Spirit to fill you with His boldness.
2. Ask the Lord to place in you the commitment of Jim Elliot.
3. Ask the Lord to give you courage when persecution comes your way.

Dear Lord,

Thank You for the courage of these missionaries to go and minister to unreached people. Thank You for the grace and mercy You gave to the missionaries' family members to go back and minister to the very people that killed their husband, father, and brother. Help us as the Church to have the boldness to share about Jesus, and help us to stand strong in the midst of any persecution we face.
In the name of Jesus, Amen.

Today's Next Step

Watch the movie "End of the Spear," the story of Jim Elliot's life.

1 Peter 5:7
Cast all your anxiety on him because he cares for you.

Many people are out of work and people are counting on their unemployment checks. They carry a lot of anxiety about tomorrow. Recently, I was in a conversation with a wealthy individual that feels anxiety and uncertainty about his business' future. I reminded this person to give that anxiety and worry over to the Lord. God cares about the birds and He feeds them, and He cares about the wildflowers that are here today and gone tomorrow. If He cares for the birds and the wildflowers, then I want to remind you how much He cares for you, whether you are worried about how you will pay bills or buy groceries or how you will keep your business going. Cast those worries on Jesus today. He's aware of your circumstances. Lean on His understanding and remember, "He cares for you."

Be honest
In what ways are the anxieties of this life currently weighing you down?

Ways to pray
1. Ask the Lord to comfort those who are unemployed and carrying anxiety.
2. Ask the Lord to comfort those whose businesses are struggling and are unsure of their futures.
3. Pray that those who are worried can truly have peace and put their complete trust in Jesus.

Dear Lord,
Please be with those whose businesses are struggling. Please comfort those who are currently unemployed and give them peace. Remind them that since You don't forget the birds or the wildflowers, You have not forgotten them either. Remind them, Jesus, how much you care about the pain they are experiencing.
In the name of Jesus, Amen.

Today's Next Step
Ask the Holy Spirit to reveal to you someone who is struggling. Pick up the phone and call them right now. Listen to them share their concerns and anxieties, and pray for them right now.

Day 26
Depression

Matthew 11:28-30
"Come to me, all you who are weary and burdened, and I will give you rest. Take my yoke upon you and learn from me, for I am gentle and humble in heart, and you will find rest for your souls. For my yoke is easy and my burden is light."

Every week I check on a few people in my neighborhood. An older lady recently lost her dog, is fighting cancer, and has no family to care for her. Another friend has several health issues and has gone through a divorce, and honestly is truly depressed. A middle-aged woman barely has enough food or money to pay her monthly bills and wonders how she will make it. People are weary and heavily burdened, and they can't carry this heaviness alone. We have to encourage them to give it over to the Lord. We must open our eyes and recognize the hurting people that the Lord has placed around us. I have come to realize that only the Lord can take away the backpacks of burdens that people are carrying, and it's our job as Christ-followers to display the love of Christ in every interaction. We must also remember that we can't stop people's depression; only Jesus is the one that can truly set them free. As we care for those who are hurting, we must remember that the most important way that we can help a person get rid of their depression is to serve them and introduce them to the love of Jesus Christ.

Be honest
In what ways are you currently feeling discouraged or seeing discouragement in our society?

Ways to pray
1. Ask the Lord to reveal to you those who are weary and carry heavy burdens.
2. Ask the Lord to point out different ways you can meet their needs and pray for them.
3. Pray that people in our nation will quit looking toward their own needs, and start looking at the needs of others.

Dear Lord,
Please help me to see those who are hurting. Give me the courage to notice and to help someone who is hurting to get back on their feet. As I obey Your leading, give me joy that brings me out of depression, so I can truly help others who are hurting.
In the name of Jesus, Amen.

Today's Next Step
If you are discouraged or depressed, call someone you trust to encourage you and pray for you. Grab a card and write a letter to someone the Lord reveals to you who may need encouragement, and send it in the mail.

Hebrews 10:24-25
And let us consider how we may spur one another on toward love and good deeds, not giving up meeting together, as some are in the habit of doing, but encouraging one another, and all the more as you see the Day approaching.

Too many of my friends have lived in isolation for way too long. If they do not get outside of their own homes and interact with others, they will end up wasting away by themselves alone. Understand that we are made to be in fellowship with people, not to live inside our homes in isolation. It's so important that we get outside, that we sit on our porches, that we invite friends over to our home. Everyone needs life-on-life interaction filled with laughter, fun, and community. Don't live in fear any longer. The Lord does not want us to live that way. He has given us power to overcome this fear that is gripping us. He also gave us the ability to love others and to help others overcome their fear. He gives us confidence to move forward with a sound mind.

Be honest
In what way do you see people living in fear? In what ways are you living in fear? How is our nation living in fear?

Ways to pray
1. Ask the Lord to give peace and joy to those who are currently gripped by fear.
2. Ask the Lord to give you a community of people to connect with, so you will not feel alone.
3. Ask the Lord to give you a sound mind to clearly be able to see the works of the evil one and push away the fear that the Lord does not want us to have.

Dear Lord,
Give me confidence; take all fear away. Help me to completely trust You, and tap into Your understanding and Your power. Help me when I am strong to help those who are weak. Give me a true community in which to share life with others. Give me strength and power to stand confidently without fear.
In the name of Jesus, Amen.

Today's Next Step
Set up a game night, a movie night, or a bonfire. Plan with the purpose to just have fun with some friends. Don't let someone's "no" to your invitation stop your planning!

Ephesians 4:31-32
Get rid of all bitterness, rage and anger, brawling and slander, along with every form of malice. Be kind and compassionate to one another, forgiving each other, just as in Christ the Lord forgave you.

My wife loves grapefruit. I personally used to hate the taste of grapefruit, and could never understand why anyone would want to spend money on this bitter-tasting fruit. I began watching my wife take extra time to peel off the outer layer and then take off the inner layer of skin. She added salt to the pieces of grapefruit, and I began to realize that I now like grapefruit. You see, you can't have bitter without sweet, and sweet without bitter. We are living in some bittersweet times. We have to deal with both the bitter and the sweet sides of the season in which we are living. We also need to get rid of our bitterness and anger toward our situation, and work toward forgiving and embracing the sweeter side of life.

Be honest
What bitterness or anger exists in you that is hurting your relationship with Jesus and the people that you love?

Ways to pray
1. Ask the Lord to rise up against the anger and bitterness in the world, and heal our world.
2. Ask the Lord to forgive our nation for its stubbornness and anger, and to fill us with kindness and compassion toward one another.
3. Ask the Lord to free you from all bitterness and allow you to see the sweet side of life and the family and friends that He has placed around you.

Dear Lord,
Rise up against the bitterness and anger in this world, and help us forgive each other just as You forgive us. Fill us as a nation with kindness and compassion for one another, and help us to see the good in the world. Help us to stand against evil, and be ready to forgive.
In the name of Jesus, Amen.

Today's Next Step
Pick one person that you have hurt with your bitterness and/or anger, and write a note or letter to apologize for the pain you have caused in his or her life, then send it.

James 5:13-16
Is anyone among you in trouble? Let them pray. Is anyone happy? Let them sing songs of praise. Is anyone among you sick? Let them call the elders of the church to pray over them and anoint them with oil in the name of the Lord. And the prayer offered in faith will make the sick person well; the Lord will raise them up. If they have sinned, they will be forgiven.

In my family many have fought diabetes, heart issues, breathing issues and even cancer. We must pray for all sickness to be gone and for healing to happen to those who are currently sick. We also must pray for the many people who are scared and living in constant fear of getting sick, and for those who are living in depression. We desperately need the Lord to work in all situations and for a true work of Jesus to heal those who are sick. Though many people have had different opinions about the COVID-19 virus, I have realized that it is real, and many have gotten sick from it. I personally have had a few friends get extremely sick, and a few others who have died from complications. I also understand the questions people have about masks, social distancing, and if this virus could also be used for political purposes or agendas. There is much conversation about this virus, but we must pray for healing to happen to those who are currently sick.

Let's not miss the opportunity to pray for one another and have faith that the Lord has the power to bring healing to those who are sick, and to forgive this nation so true healing can take place.

Be honest
Who do you know who is sick and/or fighting a chronic illness? How can you encourage them and pray for them?

Ways to pray
1. Ask the Lord to heal those who are sick, and comfort them through the recovery process.
2. Ask the Lord to give you compassion for others, to be with them through all circumstances.
3. Ask the Lord to give you courage through pain and sickness, so you can continue to do His work in the world.

Dear Lord,
I ask you to heal those who are sick and in chronic pain. Take away the fear and depression that fill so many people. Give me compassion for those who are sick, and help me continue to live with courage in this world. Show me who I need to encourage today.
In the name of Jesus, Amen.

Today's Next Step
Write down the names of people that you know personally who are sick. Ask the Lord to reveal to you which one of these people you need to call and encourage today.

Healthcare Workers

Luke 10:34
He went to him and bound up his wounds, pouring on oil and wine. Then he set him on his own animal and brought him to an inn and took care of him.

Throughout history we have always identified heroes as soldiers risking their lives to fight for our freedom, firefighters running in burning buildings to save lives, police officers protecting us, and EMTs showing up in our times of need. When we experienced the global pandemic of COVID-19, we began to recognize our healthcare workers as true heroes as well. We saw endless examples of real-life heroes, putting their lives on the line to save other lives. Early on with all the unknowns these medical professionals didn't miss a beat and took on the challenge to not only save lives, but be sources of encouragement when families could not visit patients in the hospital. I believe they not only saved people's lives medically, but they saved them emotionally as well. I have truly come to realize that these doctors, nurses, and physicians care about our health and our well-being. I am so thankful for the way the Lord is using them, and it's such an honor for us to pray for them today.

Be honest
Imagine you are a healthcare worker. Would you have had the courage to go into work knowing you were putting your life on the line?

Ways to pray
1. Ask the Lord to protect the health of our healthcare workers as they work for healing for those who are sick.
2. Ask the Lord to protect the families of healthcare workers against sickness.
3. Ask the Lord to give boldness and protection to medical professionals, and give them the strength to continue to be people of integrity.

Dear Lord,
Please continue to protect our medical professionals who risk their lives and their careers daily to save lives. Put a shield of protection around them and their families as they take care of those who are sick. Give them an extra portion of Your strength to endure the long hours and the mental stress they face on a daily basis. Bless them and strengthen them.
In the name of Jesus, Amen.

Today's Next Step
Take the time to write a note, get on social media or pick up your phone and thank a healthcare worker today. They need the encouragement.

Day 31

First Responders

Matthew 25:35-36
For I was hungry and you gave me something to eat, I was thirsty and you gave me something to drink, I was a stranger and you invited me in, I needed clothes and you clothed me, I was sick and you looked after me, I was in prison and you came to visit me.

I have been so impacted by first responders. I have watched my brother-in-law be a paramedic, police officer, and firefighter, and I have watched these professionals protect, care for, and save people's lives. When I had a concussion, I was cared for by paramedics in an ambulance, and then brought back to health by nurses in the hospital. I have had amazing police officer friends throughout the years who truly are some of the most caring people I have ever met. One such friend carried blankets in the back of his police car every night to hand out to homeless people that were cold during winters in Michigan. I have witnessed firefighters run into burning buildings and save people's lives. These people are heroes, and I don't want to miss the opportunity to recognize them and pray for them. I truly believe we need to take the time to encourage them. My dad told me this truth that I try to always live by: "If you think something good about a person, make sure that you tell them." Let's not miss the opportunity to care for those who sacrifice their lives on a daily basis for us. Thank you for caring for us and putting your lives on the line to keep us safe every day.

Be honest
When was the last time you thanked one of our first responders?

Ways to pray
1. Ask the Lord to fill the families of our first responders with peace about their loved one's safety.
2. Pray that people will encourage and thank our first responders.
3. Ask the Lord to protect our first responders and strengthen their immune systems, and to give wisdom to them as they care for people daily.

Dear Lord,
Thank You for our first responders. Please encourage them and keep them safe. Thank You for the sacrifice they make daily. Please give them extra strength and endurance to not quit, but to stay the course and continue to press on. Help us as believers to not miss the opportunity to continue to pray and encourage these heroes.
In the name of Jesus, Amen.

Today's Next Step
Make a gift basket with a personal note, and drop it off at your local fire station, police station, or another first responders' center. Thank them for their sacrifice and tell them how much you appreciate all that they do.

James 1:5
If any of you lacks wisdom, you should ask the Lord, who gives generously to all without finding fault, and it will be given to you.

I have a friend who is a teacher and is not very technically driven. He has had to learn a whole new way of teaching within the school system. Though he is close to retirement, he decided to continue teaching because he cares so much about the students he has under his care. Many teachers could have retired early or even quit, but many chose to put their desires aside and put these students above themselves. With technical difficulties daily, new on-line learning platforms, and trying to keep students' attention while at home on a computer screen, I cannot begin to imagine the challenges our educators have faced in recent months. I personally want to thank presidents, principles, professors, teachers, and parents for loving your students so much, and for working extra hours, learning new programs, and working double duty to invest in educating our children and young professionals. Your impact is not just their education, but you have been a life-on-life example of interaction and consistency that they have needed daily. You have kept our students' dreams alive and though you may never get the "thank you" that you deserve, you are a true blessing to us all. Let's not miss the opportunity to encourage our educators and pray for our schools and universities.

Be honest

Have you noticed how hard educators and institutions of learning have worked to give children an opportunity to learn?

Ways to pray

1. Ask the Lord to give wisdom to professors and teachers as they continue to adapt to new ways of teaching.
2. Ask the Lord to fill parents who are juggling work and teaching their children with peace and grace.
3. Pray for our children to get life-on-life interaction that will allow them to be socially strong and encouraged.

Dear Lord,

Give our educators strength and stamina as they teach. Give them wisdom and joy, and allow that joy to impact each student You place in their classrooms online or in-person. Give parents confidence in the decisions educators make. Encourage our students and help them to enjoy school. Allow more social opportunities to exist for our kids.
In the name of Jesus, Amen.

Today's Next Step

Get on social media today, or write a personal note, and thank a teacher, professor, or any person in education for his or her diligence and hard work.

Hebrews 13:3
Continue to remember those in prison as if you were together with them in prison, and those who are mistreated as if you yourselves were suffering.

We are called to love one another, to show hospitality to strangers, to remember those in prison as if we were with them in prison, and to understand their suffering and what they are going through. Many times people ignore those in prison because they believe they deserve punishment for the crime they have committed, so people have no mercy or grace to extend to a criminal. I often wonder what would happen if Jesus treated us the same way, and he never showed us grace, mercy, or forgiveness. If Jesus can extend us love, then we should be able to extend love to the worst of sinners. Why would we not pray for those in prison? Why would we not be willing to serve and lead Bible studies for those living on the inside? Why would we not write letters to inmates in prison to encourage them? Why would we not help prisoners' families who may be barely surviving in our current economy?

Be honest
When was the last time you truly had empathy and grace for those who are living in prison?

Ways to pray
1. Ask the Lord to give you a bigger heart to care for those who are in prison.
2. Pray for spouses of prisoners who are dealing with pain and the responsibility of keeping the bills paid, and for the children who cannot see their imprisoned parents.
3. Pray against loneliness and depression of those who are in prison.

Dear Lord,
Help me to not forget those who are suffering and hurting in prison. Give me a huge heart to sympathize with those who are mistreated and many times forgotten. I ask You to make yourself known to prisoners and help them truly understand the love and grace that You offer to them.
In the name of Jesus, Amen.

Today's Next Step
Do a Google search on ways you can help those who are in prison, or ask the Lord to reveal a family who may need some encouragement because their family member is currently in prison. Be sensitive when you call, but don't hesitate to make contact or pray for them.

Day 34

Political Divide

2 Corinthians 13:11
Finally, brothers and sisters, rejoice! Strive for full restoration, encourage one another, be of one mind, live in peace. And the God of love and peace will be with you.

There is such a divide among the Democrats and Republicans. Many of us wonder if we will ever see respect between parties and a willingness to work together in the future. We need God to intervene in this divide, and we need the presence of the Holy Spirit to heal this nation that is so divided. I pray that the hatred that abounds can move to love for one another. Both parties will never truly agree on all perspectives, but this rage and anger that boils in our culture and in these parties needs to stop. We all feel the tension that exists in our country, and we need God to bring peace, unity, and forgiveness within this political divide. The hatred, lies, deception, and fear have to stop, and Jesus, we need you to bring complete clarity and order to our lives and in our nation. Let's not miss the opportunities to encourage one another, have conversations, and respect one another even in our disagreements. Let's stand on godly principles, but also remember to love.

Be honest
Are you dividing your friends politically, or are you a voice of truth in their lives?

Ways to pray
1. Pray for the divide that exists in our Senate, House of Representatives, and political parties.
2. Pray for the Lord to eliminate the anger that currently exists in our country.
3. Pray for peace, humility, forgiveness, compassion and unity to exist again in this country.

Dear Lord,
We need Your help right now. This nation is so divided, and hate is affecting every facet of our country. People are nervous about the future and the unknowns. We need Your clarity and order to rule this nation again. Bring us to our knees, Jesus. Heal the divide, and give us wisdom when interacting with others who believe differently than us.
In the name of Jesus, Amen.

Today's Next Step
Write down three practical ways you can interact in a positive way with those who believe differently than you.

Romans 13:1-2
Let everyone be subject to the governing authorities, for there is no authority except that which the Lord has established. The authorities that exist have been established by the Lord. Consequently, whoever rebels against the authority is rebelling against what the Lord has instituted, and those who do so will bring judgment on themselves.

We are called to be subject to the governing authorities. I have not agreed with everything that our governor has issued, but that is my governing authority. Many may not agree with the president's decisions, but he has been instituted by the Lord. As much as we desire to resist these guidelines, we could be resisting what the Lord has appointed. To be completely honest, I hate to be told what to do, especially when I feel as if my freedoms are being taken away, but when I look at Scripture, it guides me to what I believe we should do during this time. Jesus teaches us to love our neighbor (Matthew 22:39) and to put others above ourselves (Philippians 2:3). In the verse above, we are told to respect those the Lord has put in authority. The Lord also tells us to love our enemies and to pray for those who persecute us (Matthew 5:44). Instead of hating those in authority, we should be praying for them.

Be honest

When was the last time you prayed for those in authority and leadership over you?

Ways to pray

1. Ask the Lord to speak to our leaders and that they will be listening for His guidance.
2. Ask the Lord to give them strength as they lead.
3. Ask the Lord to help you honor and respect those in authority over you.

Dear Lord,

Give me the strength to pray for my leaders. Give my leaders wisdom and clarity with the decisions that are ahead for my country. Help my leaders to know Jesus and to not focus on the branches of government, but help them to focus on You. Help them to be able to hear your voice, recognize it, and push away the voice of the enemy. Help me to respect those the Lord has appointed over me.
In the name of Jesus, Amen.

Today's Next Step

Find out who is in leadership and authority positions in your city and state, and pray for them by name. Write them a note of encouragement and send it. Lovingly encourage them to follow biblical truth.

Reach Out & Break Bubbles

Matthew 28:19-20
Therefore go and make disciples of all nations, baptizing them in the name of the Father and of the Son and of the Holy Spirit, and teaching them to obey everything I have commanded you. And surely I am with you always, to the very end of the age.

I went to a Christian university. In my years there, I grew in my relationship with Jesus Christ, but one day I looked around my group of friends and realized I lived in a Christian bubble. All these Christians were on campus, but just off the campus, not even a mile away, were many hurting people. The Lord broke my heart that day for those who did not know Jesus. I often wonder why Christians stay indoors. We go to church, participate in Bible studies, serve in the Church, eat at potlucks, and engage in fellowship with other Christians. We talk about reaching others outside of church, and even do outreach events to reach the unchurched. We then pat ourselves on the back because of our good deeds. What if we expanded our circle and rubbed shoulders with those who think differently than us, engaging in conversation with them? How about really getting to know our neighbors and opening our life up to them? What if we took time weekly to be missional and intentionally be in the culture where the Lord has placed us? It's time for us to break the bubble, and get out of our comfort zones. I've come to understand our lives must happen mostly outside the church.

Be honest
How do you need to break out of your Christian bubble?

Ways to pray
1. Ask the Lord to help you befriend someone who does not know Jesus.
2. Ask the Holy Spirit to truly invade your life, and keep you from becoming so religious that you stop the Holy Spirit from moving in your life.
3. Ask the Lord to help you realize right now how ripe the harvest field is, and to give you the courage to share and engage in conversation about Jesus Christ.

Dear Lord,
Help me to realize the Christian bubble in which I have placed myself. Give me the courage to expand my circle and go beyond my comfort zone. Help me to not remain inside, but go beyond the walls I have built up around me. Lord, please break my Christian bubble and help me begin to have conversations with others who are different than me. Allow me to step out in order to grow my faith even more.
In the name of Jesus, Amen.

Today's Next Step
Pick up your phone and scroll through your contacts. Ask the Lord to reveal to you which person you need to call and share about what Jesus has done in your life. As you step out in obedience, the Lord will use your story to connect that person with Jesus. Don't be afraid to find out where they are spiritually, and ask them to commit their life to Christ.

Ephesians 5:15-17
Be very careful, then, how you live—not as unwise but as wise, making the most of every opportunity, because the days are evil. Therefore do not be foolish, but understand what the Lord's will is.

Recently I led the funeral of a man who was 42-years-old and died of a massive heart attack. I was reminded how short life is. I started thinking about how important today is and how many times we take each day for granted. You see, we can get so focused on circumstances, or be frozen in fear of the unknown, that we miss out on the opportunity we have right now to notice the blessings of our faith, our children, and the amazing ways Jesus has provided for us. The verse above tells us to make the most of every opportunity. This is our opportunity to live wisely. Seize this season the Lord has placed you in, and embrace the moments the Lord has given to you this day.

Be honest
In what ways are you missing the opportunities and blessings the Lord has put before you?

Ways to pray
1. Ask the Lord to help you live wisely and see the blessings in this season in which He has placed you.
2. Ask the Lord to reveal to you the opportunities He has for you to minister and care for the needs of others.
3. Ask the Lord to give you an opportunity today to bring hope into someone's life that is living in fear of the unknown.

Dear Lord,
Give me wisdom in how I live, and help me not to miss the blessings and opportunities that you have for me today. Help me embrace each day and not just see the clouds, but help me also to see the sunshine. Help me bring joy to someone's life today that is fearful about tomorrow.
In the name of Jesus, Amen.

Today's Next Step
Count the number of months until your child leaves for college, and make the most of those months you have left. Put a reminder in your phone daily to not miss the opportunity to encourage your spouse, child, family member, or best friend.

Day 38

Planting Seeds

Luke 8:11-15

"This is the meaning of the parable: The seed is the word of the Lord. Those along the path are the ones who hear, and then the devil comes and takes away the word from their hearts, so that they may not believe and be saved. Those on the rocky ground are the ones who receive the word with joy when they hear it, but they have no root. They believe for a while, but in the time of testing they fall away. The seed that fell among thorns stands for those who hear, but as they go on their way they are choked by life's worries, riches and pleasures, and they do not mature. But the seed on good soil stands for those with a noble and good heart, who hear the word, retain it, and by persevering produce a crop."

In this parable, a farmer goes out, plants seeds, and they fall on four different soils. These four soils represent each of us when we give our lives to Christ. Most of the seeds fall on bad soil and don't produce a harvest. Some seeds fall on the good soil and produce a harvest larger than imagined. Many times we don't see the fruit of our seeds and we can get discouraged, feeling as if we shouldn't share the Lord's love any longer. I have come to realize that our job is to keep planting seeds everywhere and never stop sharing about the message of Jesus. We can't worry about seeds that don't produce. In the midst of everything, we must trust the Lord in all things, lean on his understanding, submit to him, and he will direct us (Proverbs 3:5-6). We must step out of our comfort zones, and let people know about Jesus. This is the time for us to encourage, care for people, help others, and share about the hope we have in Jesus Christ. When people are gripped with fear, we bring them true peace and joy. When people are worried, we remind them how much Jesus cares about them. When people are searching, we don't miss the opportunities to engage in conversation and plant seeds that can produce an abundant harvest, changing the course of their lives forever!

Be honest
What makes you hesitate to share about Jesus Christ?

Ways to pray
1. Ask the Lord to use you to share about Jesus.
2. Ask the Lord to help you see the opportunities he places in front of you each day.
3. Pray for boldness to share Jesus in challenging times.

Dear Lord,
Please give me an urgency to share about You. Help me to not live in fear, but to trust that You are working, and You are giving me opportunities and moments daily to share about Your amazing grace. Help me to not miss the opportunities to spread seeds everywhere.
In the name of Jesus, Amen.

Today's Next Step
Write on social media asking for prayer requests, then actually take the time to pray and respond to each request.

Day 39

Stand Up, Church!

2 Chronicles 7:14
If my people, who are called by my name, will humble themselves and pray and seek my face and turn from their wicked ways, then I will hear from heaven, and I will forgive their sins and will heal their land.

Abraham Lincoln fought slavery and helped a nation change. Martin Luther King, Jr. stood up against segregation. The Tank Man, the "unknown rebel," stood in front of 59 military Chinese tanks at Tiananmen Square in 1989, holding off their attack. The boldness of these historic figures inspires all of us. They are the people about whom we continue to talk. In the Bible, David, a young boy, stood up against a giant named Goliath. Three Hebrew boys would not bow down to a golden statue. Daniel was told not to pray, yet he did, and was tossed into a den of lions. Moses stood up against Pharaoh. Stephen was the first martyr. Paul was beaten for the cause of Christ. And now more than ever before, our Christian beliefs are being challenged every day. Most of us are silent and just let it all happen. It's time for the Church to be an army that rises up and takes a stand, like those in history and the many examples we read about in the Bible. It's about us coming together and being vocal about our love for Jesus Christ and the people around us. I am one small voice, but with many small voices, we can become the shout of an army. It's not about standing as a political party, but as Christ-followers standing for the Lord's truth.

Be honest

In what ways have you stood up boldly for your faith in Jesus? In what ways could you be more bold?

Ways to pray

1. Ask for the Lord's will to be accomplished, whatever the outcome.
2. Ask the Lord to give you boldness to stand up for Him.
3. Ask the Lord to forgive our sins, heal our land, and protect this nation from the dangers of the evil one, giving each of us wisdom as we live our day-to-day lives.

Dear Lord,

On behalf of our nation, we humble ourselves before You, and we realize we have allowed sin to enter. We make a decision right now to wholeheartedly seek Your face and turn from the wickedness of sin that has been entangling this nation. We confess our sin to You and repent. We ask You to forgive our sin and restore us back to You. Protect us from evil and help us put Your armor on daily. Help us be prepared for the battle we are in right now.
In the name of Jesus, Amen.

Today's Next Step

Ask God to reveal to you how you can be more bold in your faith. Write down three ways you plan to step out of your comfort zone by showing the love of Christ within the next week.

James 5:16
Therefore confess your sins to each other and pray for each other so that you may be healed. The prayer of a righteous person is powerful and effective.

William Carey, a missionary to India, once said, "Prayer - secret, fervent, believing prayer - lies at the root of all personal godliness." In 1857, the Great Awakening started with three men from New York praying daily. Then there were five men. A week later, there were fourteen men gathering daily to pray for their nation to wake up. In only eight months, fifty thousand people were saved in New York City, and the revival had spread across the entire United States. It then spread across the world. It is said that even people on ships approaching the coast could feel the convicting power of the Holy Spirit, and were saved and filled with joy even before they reached land. What would it look like to have a revival again in the world? One thing we do know, it has to start on our knees, praying with all our might. Corrie ten Boom, who helped Jews escape the Nazis during World War II, stated, "Don't pray when you feel like it. Have an appointment with the Lord and keep it. A man is powerful on his knees."

Be honest
How do you see God currently moving in your life?
How do you see God moving in our nation?

Ways to pray
1. Ask the Lord to help you be devoted to prayer and to keeping a daily appointment with him.
2. Ask the Lord to change our community and this nation, and to use the Church more than ever before.
3. Pray for a great revival and awakening to hit this world in a powerful way.

Dear Lord,
Help my prayer life and passion for You to increase. Help me to have an appointment set up with You daily that will not be interrupted, and let it be a time that I cherish. Help my prayers to be powerful and effective. Help me to do war on the floor and have my prayer be so constant that my knees begin to hurt. Bring this nation back to You, and start a revival in us to transform this world.
In the name of Jesus, Amen.

Today's Next Step
Commit to praying daily for revival, both in your own life and in our nation.

AFTER 40 DAYS

Awake

Reflect on Your Journey

You have spent forty days praying, fasting, listening, journaling, and embracing this prayer devotional. Spend some time reflecting and writing down what the Lord has taught you from this time with Him.

In what ways have you grown closer to the Lord?

In what ways have you been awakened spiritually?

In what ways has your prayer life grown?

In what ways will you continue to get closer to the Lord because of this experience?

If you want to share your experience with the author, please e-mail *info@awake40days.com*

A Final Prayer of Commitment

Dear Lord,

As a Christ-follower called by Your name, I humble myself, seek Your face, and turn from wickedness (2 Chronicles 7:14). I follow Your truth, I repent of my wrongs and am equipped for Your work. I am not like the world, my mind is renewed, and I discern Your will for my life (Romans 12:2). I will let my light shine powerfully and expose the darkness (John 1:5). I choose to throw off all hindrances that slow me down and remove any sins that entangle me. I will run with perseverance (Hebrews 12:1). My outside matches my inside (Matthew 23:28). I obey Your truth. I am an imitator of You and push away temptation (1 Peter 1:14-16). I am awake spiritually, and You shine through me. I live carefully, walk with wisdom, and see opportunities to share. I run away from evil (Ephesians 5:15-16). My heart is pure, my relationship with You is solid, and You live in me. (Psalms 51:10-13).

My anchor is firm and secure (Hebrews 6:19), and my foundation is built on Your bedrock to withstand all storms (Matthew 7:24-27). You have given me courage to stand and press forward through persecution (James 1:3). You live in me (John 20:22), and You direct me (Galatians 5:25). I choose to trust, submit to You always, and lean on Your understanding (Proverbs 3:5-6). I will not worry (Luke 12:25) or be controlled by fear. I trust in Your power and love, and will use the sound mind You have given me (2 Timothy 1:7).

I will sharpen others and be sharpened (Proverbs 27:17). I will help pick up those who fall (Ecclesiastes 4:9-10). I will spread the gospel and make disciples wherever You place me (Matthew 28:19-20). I rejoice in my freedom, strive for restoration, and encourage others. I walk in peace and unity with You. I am strong in You, and I am clothed with Your armor to fight the tricks of the evil one (Ephesians 6:10-18). I live for Heaven and feel confident when I stand before You (Revelations 20:11-15). I am unashamed of the gospel (Romans 1:16). I am a warrior for You. I am alert, aware, and ready. I am spiritually prepared (Mark 13:32-37).

In the name of Jesus, Amen.

Other Ways to be Involved

Pray
Ask God to impact others as they read, process, and pray through each day of this book.

Order Books to Give to Friends
If you desire to purchase hard-cover copies of this book, either for yourself, or to give to others, search "Awake 40 days" on Amazon.

Share This Resource
If you enjoyed this devotional, loan it to a friend on the Kindle app, purchase a hard copy to give to them as a gift, or send them the Amazon link to purchase it. Check out the AWAKE website (www.awake40days.com) and find out more information about this *AWAKE: 40 Days of Prayer* devotional, and future *40 Days* materials.